Introduction

In your hands, you hold a surefire way to engage even the most reluctant learners and build the reading comprehension skills all students need to succeed. Using the 40 short, high-interest passages in this book, each paired with a graphic organizer that supports its text structure, you'll find an easy way to help students learn how to find the main idea, understand cause and effect, compare and contrast, sequence events, and more. The ready-to-use Notebook files on the enclosed CD contain companion activities that make it easy to model these essential reading comprehension skills on your SMART Board. Following your lead, students can write, highlight, and underline key text right on the board.

About the Graphic Organizers

Many students are visual learners and can benefit greatly from using graphic organizers with their reading. Graphic organizers are especially helpful in identifying and sorting information. Different types of graphic organizers are particularly suited to certain types of text structures:

* **Concept webs** focus on main ideas and supporting details.
* **Sequence webs** focus on sequential events or steps in a process.
* **Venn diagrams** focus on making comparisons.
* **Charts** focus on classifying information.
* **Cause-and-effect maps** focus on identifying relationships between events.

As students complete a graphic organizer, they do the following:

* create a visual product based on their reading
* engage in understanding information from a passage
* see relationships among words, facts, and ideas
* gain a sense of purpose and control over their reading
* learn to paraphrase what they read

Point out that there is often more than one way to group information from a passage. Encourage students to fill in graphic organizers using their own words and phrases. (See the example on page 4.)

TEACHER TIPS

* Suggest that students read the passage all the way through to get the general idea. Then they can reread it to identify the information needed in the organizer.
* If students are unfamiliar with a graphic organizer, model its use before assigning the page. Think aloud as you read the passage, directions, and questions, and as you fill in the organizer.
* Because of the limited amount of space on each page, you may want to make enlarged copies of some graphic organizers for students to use. You may also suggest that they draw larger versions of the graphic organizers on separate sheets of paper.
* Use the MORE! activities found at the end of each reproducible graphic organizer page to extend and expand students' learning.

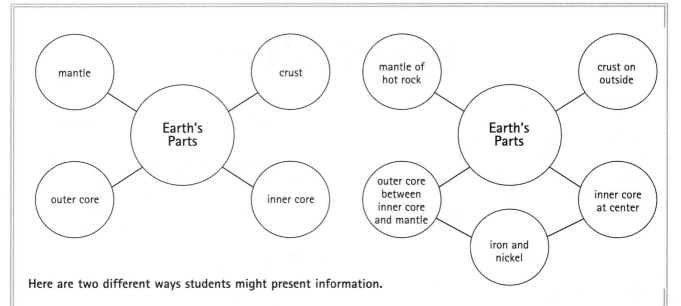

Here are two different ways students might present information.

The set of activities for each type of graphic organizer progresses from easier, offering students more support, to more challenging, allowing students greater independence. For instance the first concept web (page 6) includes the topic and one detail. The final concept web (page 14), however, requires students to decide what the paragraph topic is and to identify all six examples that tell about the topic. The activities in between are scaffolded to provide an appropriate level of challenge for a range of skill levels.

No matter their skill level, by building graphic organizers, students are more likely to understand and retain information for reports, quizzes, tests, and discussions. Each section of the book concludes with a page called Testing It Out, which is set up as a typical bubble-style test. The test questions are always based on the passage on the preceding page. Students can easily see the relationship between creating a graphic organizer and using that information on a test.

How to Use the CD and Interactive Whiteboard

On the CD, you'll find five Notebook files that correspond to each section of the book and focus on a different type of graphic organizer. There is also a pdf version of the book, which allows you to make high-quality printouts of the reproducible pages for students.

As soon as possible, transfer all of the Notebook files into a folder on the computer that is connected to your interactive whiteboard. Taking care of this step in advance saves valuable class time and also helps you when you want to saved edited samples for future reference. The CD that comes with the book will always be your master copy.

INTERACTIVE WHITEBOARD ACTIVITIES ON CD

■ SCHOLASTIC

GRADES 2–3

Short Reading Passages With Graphic Organizers

TO MODEL & TEACH KEY COMPREHENSION SKILLS

Linda Ward Beech

Edited by Mela Ottaiano
Cover design by Brian LaRossa / Interior design by Sydney Wright
Interior illustrations by Maxie Chambliss
Interactive whiteboard activities developed by Adam Hyman and designed by Brian LaRossa

ISBN-13: 978-0-545-23455-9 / ISBN-10: 0-545-23455-7

1 2 3 4 5 6 7 8 9 10   40   17 16 15 14 13 12 11 10

New York • Toronto • London • Auckland • Sydney
Mexico City • New Delhi • Hong Kong • Buenos Aires

Teaching Resources

Contents

Simply choose the lesson with the skill that you want to teach. Open the appropriate file on your interactive whiteboard and scroll to the lesson. Each lesson is comprised of 2 slides:

✳ a text-only slide featuring the paragraph
✳ a graphic organizer slide

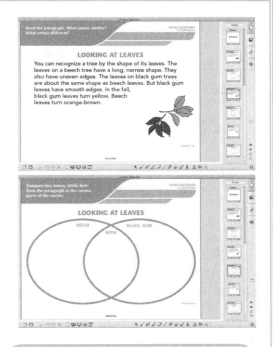

It is a good idea to preview the lesson on your computer so that you fully understand the lesson as well as the best way to convey it to students on the interactive whiteboard.

One strategy you may find helpful is to use the colored pens in the interactive whiteboard's pen tray to help students who are visual learners. For example, circling, underlining, or highlighting the main idea of a passage in green and all of the supporting details in blue is a great way to organize information by color. For consistency, use the same colors to represent a concept when completing the graphic organizers. This will also help students who are filling in the graphic organizer quickly identify key information if they need to refer back to the paragraph slide.

The final slide in each file contains an interactive version of the Testing It Out page.

Other Suggestions

✳ Be sure to use the activities that work best for the ability levels in your classroom.
✳ Encourage students to explain their thinking as they complete the organizers.
✳ Have students work in cooperative groups to complete some activities. Assign roles such as reader (one who reads the passage to the group), highlighter (one who highlights relevant parts of the passage), mapper (one who fills in the graphic organizer), and checker (one who reviews the completed graphic organizer to be sure it is correct). Encourage group members to switch roles.

⊚ TEACHER TIPS ⊚

✳ While the interactive whiteboard lessons are perfect for whole-group learning, you can also use the activities on the CD for mini-lessons, small-group instruction, differentiated instruction, and enrichment. The additional lessons can be printed or photocopied for in-class practice, homework, and assessment.

✳ As you model how to use a graphic organizer, pass out reproducible versions of the activity you choose to display, along with colored pencils, pens, or highlighters. Ask students to mark up their own copies as they follow along.

✳ To extend learning invite students to continue building onto the graphic organizer with additional information they may already know.

Fancy Fireworks

Kaboom! It's the Fourth of July. Fireworks light up the night. Have you ever seen a willow firework? It has long trails of color that float to the ground. The pinwheel and comet are two other popular fireworks. One of the loudest fireworks is called the salute. After a bright flash, you hear a loud BOOM!

Read the paragraph. Then answer the questions.

1. Which firework has long trails of color? _____

2. Which firework makes a loud BOOM? _____

3. What is a popular firework? _____

Add three more details to the web.

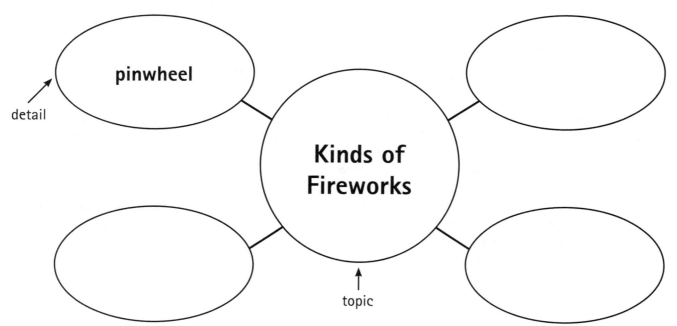

detail — pinwheel

Kinds of Fireworks

topic

MORE! What do you think a pinwheel firework looks like? Draw a picture to show your ideas.

Short Reading Passages With Graphic Organizers, Grades 2–3   Scholastic Teaching Resources

Name _____   Date _____

Things to Do in Maine

Maine has 2,500 lakes and ponds for summer fun. There are more than 400 islands along the coast. People swim, fish, and sail off these islands. Visitors enjoy eating in Maine, too. The state grows most of the blueberries in the United States. In Maine, you can eat blueberry pie and lobster all summer long!

Read the paragraph. Then answer the questions.

1. What does Maine have along its coast? _____

2. What fruit does Maine grow? _____

3. What other food is Maine known for? _____

Add three more details to the web.

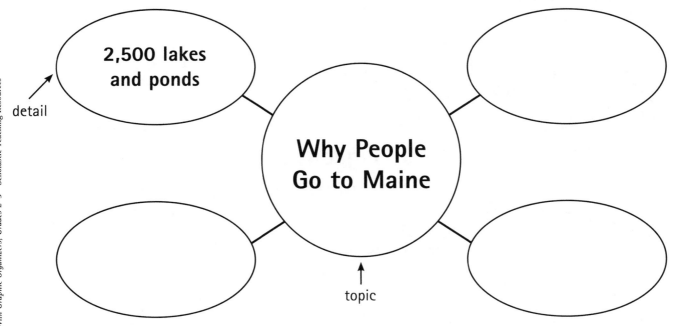

detail

2,500 lakes and ponds

Why People Go to Maine

topic

MORE! Find Maine on a map of the United States.

Short Reading Passages With Graphic Organizers, Grades 2–3 Scholastic Teaching Resources

Picture a Pigeon

What's a city bird like? Many of the birds that live in cities are pigeons. These birds are usually found on city sidewalks and on building rooftops. A pigeon weighs about half a pound. It can fly up to 60 miles an hour. Most pigeons live for 10 to 15 years.

Read the paragraph. Then answer the questions.

1. How much does a pigeon weigh? _____

2. How fast can a pigeon fly? _____

3. How long does a pigeon live? _____

Add three more details to the web.

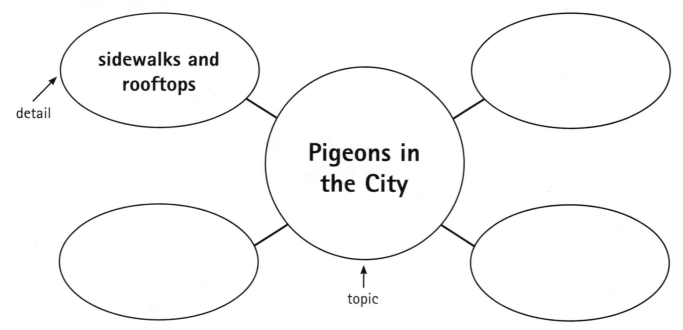

sidewalks and rooftops

detail

Pigeons in the City

topic

MORE! Baby pigeons are called squabs. Add this fact to the web.

Short Reading Passages With Graphic Organizers, Grades 2–3 Scholastic Teaching Resources

The Inside Story

You live on the outside of Earth. This part of our planet is called the crust. What is the inside of Earth like? Just below the crust is the mantle. It is made up of hot rock. Next comes the outer core. The inner core is the very center of Earth. Both the outer and inner cores are made of two minerals—iron and nickel.

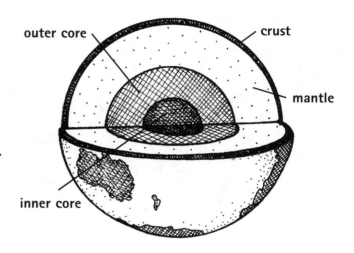

Read the topic in the web. Find four details in the paragraph that tell about the topic. Add them to the web.

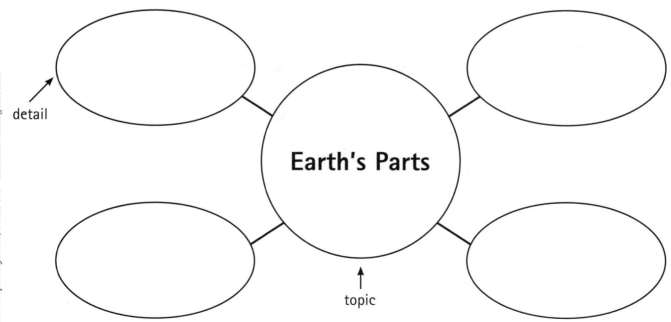

detail

Earth's Parts

topic

MORE! Use the web to tell someone about the different parts of Earth.

State Stuff

SOUTH
CAROLINA

Each state in the United States has an official flag and flower. Here are more fun facts about some states. In Arizona, the state colors are blue and gold. South Carolina's state amphibian is the salamander. Milk is the state drink in North Dakota. Maine has a state insect—the honeybee. What's the Massachusetts state dessert? It's Boston cream pie, of course!

Read the topic in the web. Find five details in the paragraph that tell about the topic. Add them to the web.

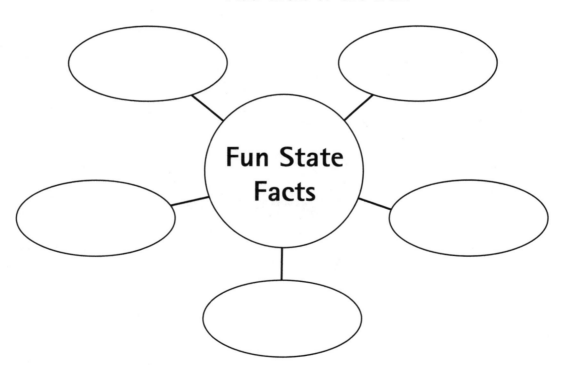

Fun State
Facts

MORE! Find out the following facts about your state: flower, nickname, bird, and one more fun fact. Make a web for your state.

A Fast Laugh

When you laugh, air comes out of your mouth at 16 miles per hour (mph). The air in a yawn can measure 9 mph. The air in a snore can be 6 to 7 mph. Air really moves when you hiccup. It can go 50 miles per hour! What's the air speed of a sneeze? It's 104 mph. Ah-choo! That's faster than the wind in a hurricane!

Read the topic in the web. Find five details in the paragraph that tell about the topic. Add them to the web.

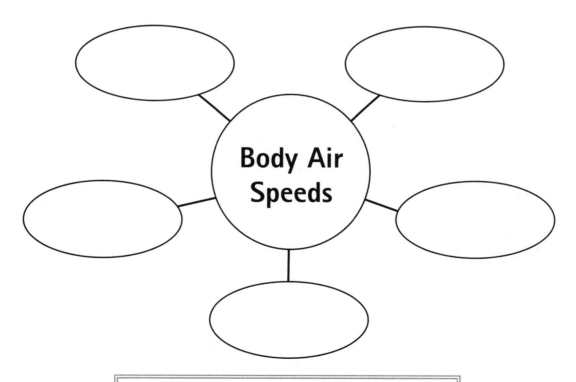

MORE!	Make a bar graph. Use the information in the paragraph.

What's for Lunch?

Have you ever had a string bean sandwich? Most students wouldn't want that for lunch! What is the favorite sandwich in America's school lunches? If you said peanut butter and jelly, you'd be right. Other popular sandwiches are ham and bologna. Cheese is the fourth favorite sandwich. Many students also like turkey sandwiches.

What is the topic of the paragraph? Write it in the center circle. Find five details that tell about the topic. Write them in the web.

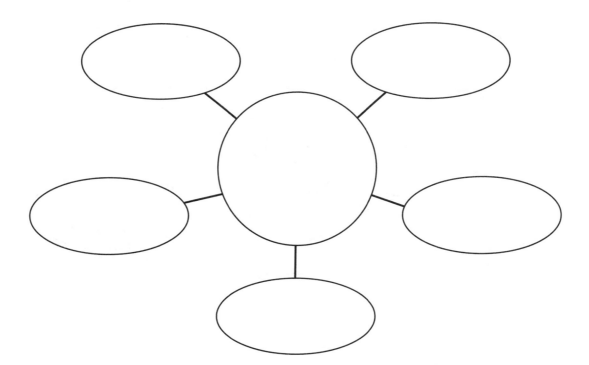

MORE! What kinds of sandwiches does your class like the best? Take a survey of your class.

Short Reading Passages With Graphic Organizers, Grades 2–3 Scholastic Teaching Resources

So Many Symbols

A symbol is a picture or object that stands for something else. For example, the American flag stands for the United States. Uncle Sam is another U.S. symbol. The name comes from the initials U.S. Have you seen the Statue of Liberty? The statue is a symbol for our country and government. The Liberty Bell stands for our freedom. Another symbol, the bald eagle, also stands for freedom.

What is the topic of the paragraph? Write it in the center circle. Find five details that tell about the topic. Write them in the web.

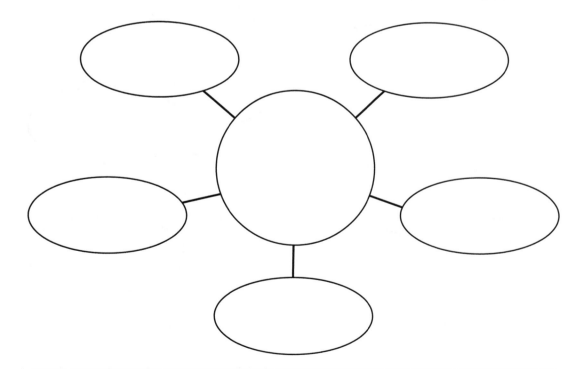

MORE! Another U.S. symbol is the Great Seal. Add this fact to the web. Find out what the Great Seal stands for.

Tracking Trains

Trains carry just about everything. Different kinds of train cars carry different things. The locomotive pulls the train. It carries the engineer, or driver. A hopper car carries things like coal, sand, and salt. A flatcar carries large things like telephone poles. The poles must be tied down. Gas is carried in a tanker car. A boxcar can hold many things, from animals to toys. The caboose is at the end of the train. It holds offices and beds for the crew.

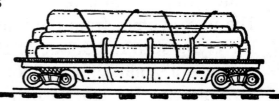

What is the topic of the paragraph? Write it in the center circle. Find six details that tell about the topic. Write them in the web.

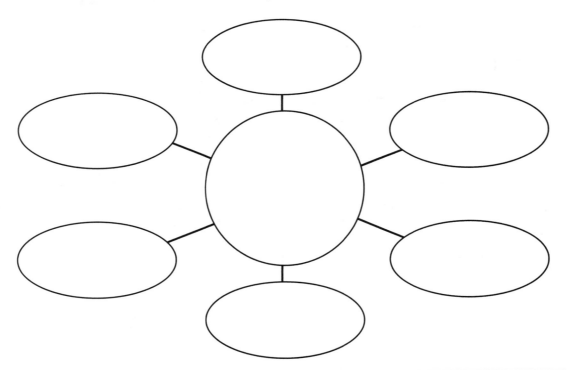

MORE! The paragraph describes a freight train. Find out what the word *freight* means. Write a sentence using the word.

Short Reading Passages With Graphic Organizers, Grades 2–3 Scholastic Teaching Resources

Testing It Out

Use after completing Tracking Trains on page 14.
Fill in the circle of the best answer.

1. The main idea of the paragraph is that—
- Ⓐ boxcars hold many different kinds of things
- Ⓑ different train cars carry different things
- Ⓒ the locomotive is the most important car
- Ⓓ a train has six different kinds of cars

2. A train car that carries sand is a—
- Ⓐ locomotive
- Ⓑ hopper
- Ⓒ boxcar
- Ⓓ caboose

3. The last car in a freight train is the—
- Ⓐ locomotive
- Ⓑ caboose
- Ⓒ hopper
- Ⓓ tanker

4. You can guess that a flatcar can carry—
- Ⓐ big pipes
- Ⓑ gas
- Ⓒ sand
- Ⓓ pigs

5. A tanker might carry—
- Ⓐ animals
- Ⓑ logs
- Ⓒ the crew
- Ⓓ oil

6. The most powerful car on a freight train must be the—
- Ⓐ tanker
- Ⓑ locomotive
- Ⓒ flatcar
- Ⓓ caboose

7. On long trips, the engineer probably sleeps in the—
- Ⓐ boxcar
- Ⓑ locomotive
- Ⓒ caboose
- Ⓓ tanker

8. Piles of wheat would be carried in a—
- Ⓐ hopper
- Ⓑ locomotive
- Ⓒ flatcar
- Ⓓ boxcar

Short Reading Passages With Graphic Organizers, Grades 2–3 Scholastic Teaching Resources

Hello, Island!

About 30 years ago, some fishermen were on their boat near Iceland. Suddenly they saw smoke coming from the sea. Then the top of a volcano rose out of the water. Soon red-hot rock began to pour down its sides. It looked like the sea was on fire. At last the volcano cooled down. It became a new island. People named the island Surtsey.

Read how the island of Surtsey was made. Show the correct order of what happened. Write the numbers from 1–4 on the lines.

_____ Red-hot rock poured down its sides.

_____ Smoke came out of the sea.

_____ The new island was named Surtsey.

_____ The volcano cooled down.

Fill in the circles in order. Use the numbers and sentences above to help you. The first one is done for you.

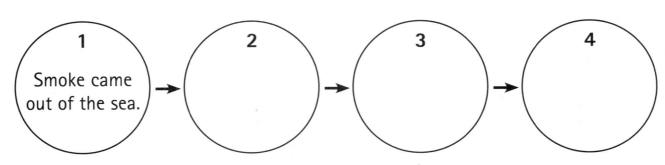

1
Smoke came out of the sea. → 2 → 3 → 4

MORE! Tell someone how Surtsey became an island. Draw pictures to show what happened.

Short Reading Passages With Graphic Organizers, Grades 2–3 Scholastic Teaching Resources

Turn on the Lights

Lighthouses warn ships that are near land. The first lighthouses were fires. People would build the fires on hilltops along the coast. Later, people built towers. The light from their candles could be seen from far away. Then oil lamps were used. Today electricity runs a lighthouse's powerful lamps.

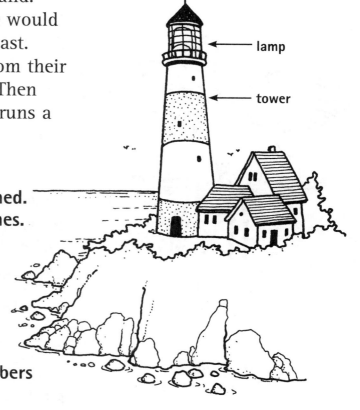

**Read how lighthouses changed.
Show the correct order of what happened.
Write the numbers from 1–4 on the lines.**

_____ Oil lamps lit lighthouses.

_____ Lighthouses use electric light.

_____ Fires were built on hillsides.

_____ Candles were used.

Fill in the circles in order. Use the numbers and sentences above to help you.

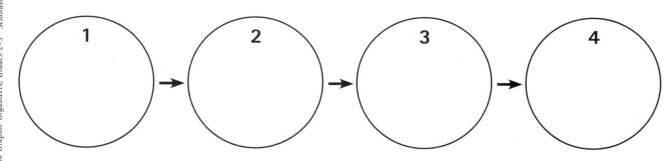

MORE! Read *The Little Red Lighthouse and the Great Gray Bridge* by Hildegarde Swift.

Here Come the Cranes

About half a million sandhill cranes cover the sky. Every March, these large birds come to the Platte River in Nebraska. The river is an important stop on the birds' trip north. For about six weeks, the cranes rest and eat there. Then, as the spring breezes turn warm, the birds leave. They head for the far north. The cranes' mating season begins there.

Read about the sandhill cranes' trip.
Show the correct order of what happens.
Write the numbers from 1–4 on the lines.

_____ The cranes fly to the far north.

_____ The mating season begins.

_____ The cranes eat and rest.

_____ The cranes come to the Platte River.

Fill in the circles in order. Use the numbers and sentences above to help you.

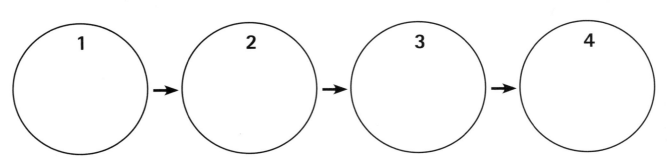

| MORE! | The sandhill cranes fly to the Platte River from the Gulf of Mexico. Add this fact to the web. |

Short Reading Passages With Graphic Organizers, Grades 2–3 Scholastic Teaching Resources

A Painted Cave

A very long time ago, people lived in caves. Here's how four boys found some very old cave paintings in France. They were out with their dog Robot. Suddenly the boys couldn't find Robot. Then they heard the dog barking—under the ground! The boys climbed down a hole to find Robot. They also found a cave with paintings on its walls and ceiling. Someone had painted them over 15,000 years ago! Today these cave paintings are famous.

Read about how the cave paintings were found. Show the correct order of what happened. Write the numbers from 1–5 on the lines.

_____ Robot gets lost.

_____ The boys hear barking and climb into a hole.

_____ The boys find cave paintings.

_____ Four boys go out with their dog.

_____ The cave paintings become very famous.

Fill in the circles in order. Use the numbers and sentences above to help you.

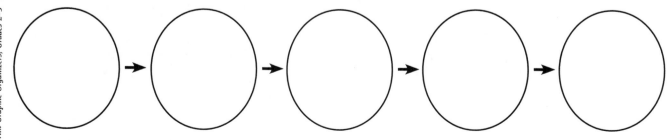

MORE! Suppose you could ask each of the four boys a question. What would you ask them?

Easy Opening

In 1959, the Fraze family was on a picnic. They had forgotten to bring a can opener. Mr. Fraze finally opened the can on the bumper of his car. "There must be a better way," he said. One night, Mr. Fraze invented the pop-top can. About 20 years later, he invented the push-in, fold-back top. It's still in use today.

Complete the sequence web. Show the correct order of what happened. The first one is done for you.

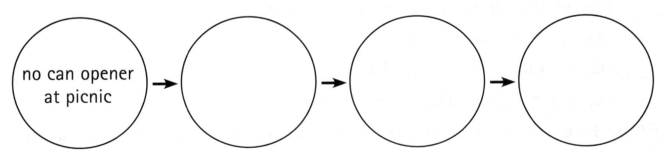

no can opener at picnic →   →   →

MORE! Ermal Fraze was from Dayton, Ohio. Find this city on a United States map.

Short Reading Passages With Graphic Organizers, Grades 2–3 Scholastic Teaching Resources

Toys Through Time

Some toys have been around for a long time. Others are much newer. One of the earliest toys is the whistle. Many Native American children had whistles. The rocking horse is about 200 years old. Crayons have been around for about 100 years. Video games are fairly new. The first one came out about 40 years ago, in 1970. The first bike was made 150 years ago.

Complete the sequence web. Show the order in which toys were first used.

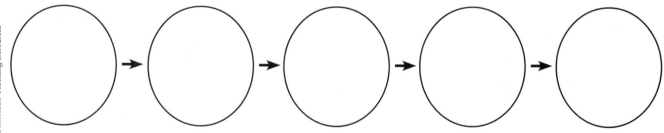

The Frisbee is about 70 years old. Where would that go on the web?

Short Reading Passages With Graphic Organizers, Grades 2–3 Scholastic Teaching Resources

Balloons on Parade

Many people enjoy the big balloons at the Thanksgiving Day parade in New York City. Here's how these balloons are made. First drawings of what the balloon might look like are done. Next, small models are created. Then workers cut out and put together the pieces for the big balloon. Finally the balloon is blown up and painted.

Complete the sequence web. Show the order in which parade balloons are made.

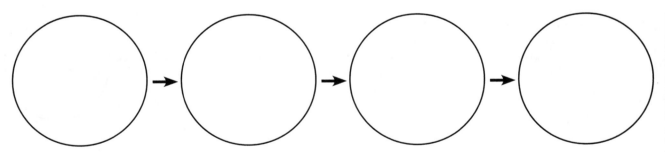

MORE! Draw your own parade balloon.

Testing It Out

Use after completing Balloons on Parade on page 22.
Fill in the circle of the best answer.

1. The first step in making a parade balloon is—
- Ⓐ making models
- Ⓑ blowing it up
- Ⓒ doing drawings
- Ⓓ painting it

2. After the balloon is blown up, it is—
- Ⓐ cheered by crowds
- Ⓑ popped
- Ⓒ put in a parade
- Ⓓ painted

3. The models of the balloon are—
- Ⓐ large
- Ⓑ small
- Ⓒ 5 feet tall
- Ⓓ 500 feet tall

4. The balloon pieces are cut out—
- Ⓐ before the drawings are done
- Ⓑ before the balloon is blown up
- Ⓒ after they are painted
- Ⓓ after the parade begins

5. The models are important because they—
- Ⓐ are made before the drawings are done
- Ⓑ appear in the parade
- Ⓒ are put inside the balloon
- Ⓓ show what the balloon will look like

6. The paragraph suggests that making a parade balloon—
- Ⓐ is easy
- Ⓑ takes time
- Ⓒ is done by one person
- Ⓓ is a sad job

7. The paragraph does <u>not</u> tell you—
- Ⓐ where the Thanksgiving Day Parade is
- Ⓑ when the balloon is painted
- Ⓒ where the balloons are kept during the year
- Ⓓ which parade the balloon is for

8. You can guess that the balloons are—
- Ⓐ easy to carry
- Ⓑ used all year
- Ⓒ very small
- Ⓓ made carefully

On the Ferry

You're in a car. You come to a big lake. There's no bridge. How do you get across? In some places, you can take a boat called a ferry. A car ferry has ramps so you can drive onto the boat. Some ferries are for trains. These boats have tracks on them. Both kinds of ferries are about 330 feet long.

Read the paragraph. Then answer the questions.

1. What is the job of each kind of ferry? _____

2. How long are most ferryboats? _____

3. Which kind of ferry has tracks? _____

4. Which kind of ferry has ramps? _____

Write your answers in the correct parts of the circles.

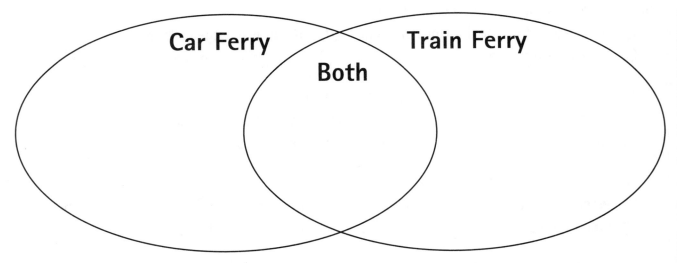

Car Ferry   Both   Train Ferry

MORE! Planes can land on some ships. Find out what these ships are called.

Short Reading Passages With Graphic Organizers, Grades 2–3 Scholastic Teaching Resources

Looking at Leaves

Black Gum

Beech

You can recognize a tree by the shape of its leaves. The leaves on a beech tree have a long, narrow shape. They also have uneven edges. The leaves on black gum trees are about the same shape as beech leaves. But black gum leaves have smooth edges. In the fall, black gum leaves turn yellow. Beech leaves turn orange-brown.

Read the paragraph. Then answer the questions.

1. What are the edges of each kind of leaf like? _____

2. What color does each kind of leaf turn? _____

3. What shape are the leaves on both trees? _____

Write your answers in the correct parts of the circles.

Beech   **Both**   **Black Gum**

MORE! Find leaves from two different trees. Make a diagram like the one on this page. Fill in the diagram to show how the leaves are alike and different.

Short Reading Passages With Graphic Organizers, Grades 2–3   Scholastic Teaching Resources

Foreign Flags

Every country has its own flag. Japan has a white flag with a red circle on it. The red circle stands for the sun. Japan's name means the "land of the rising sun." Canada also has a red and white flag. But its flag has a white background with two wide red stripes. In the center of the flag is a red maple leaf. The maple tree is a symbol of Canada.

Read the paragraph. Then answer the questions.

1. What colors are both flags? _____

2. What does Japan's flag have in the center? _____

3. What does Canada's flag have in the center? _____

4. How are the backgrounds of the two flags different? _____

Write your answers in the correct parts of the circles.

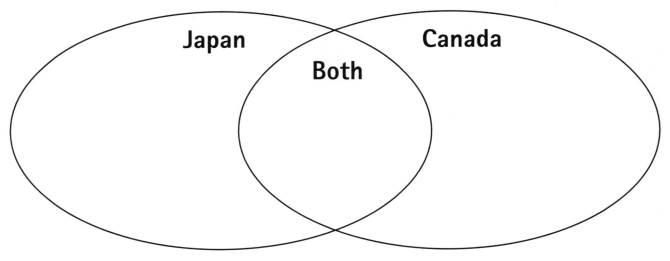

MORE! Find Japan and Canada on a world map.

Short Reading Passages With Graphic Organizers, Grades 2–3 Scholastic Teaching Resources

Opposite Poles

The South Pole is on the continent of Antarctica. Where is the North Pole? It's in the middle of the Arctic Ocean. There is no land at the North Pole—just slabs of ice. Both poles are very cold places. Both have six months of daylight and six months of darkness. People don't make their homes on either pole, but scientists do work on Antarctica. They study the ice and rocks there.

Read the paragraph. Write facts in each part of the Venn diagram.

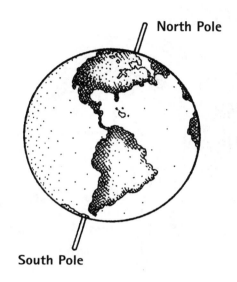

North Pole

South Pole

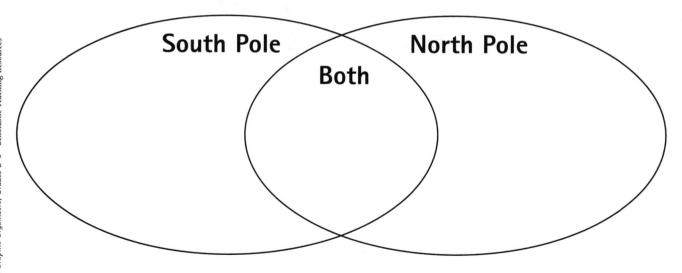

South Pole   **North Pole**

Both

MORE! When it is dark at the North Pole, it is light at the South Pole. Find out why this is so.

A State Apart

The state of Michigan has two parts—
the Upper Peninsula and the Lower
Peninsula. Peninsulas are long arms
of land that jut into water. Both of
Michigan's peninsulas are almost
surrounded by the Great Lakes. The
Upper Peninsula has many big forests.
It is also rich in minerals. The Lower
Peninsula has more people and large
cities. Most of the state's industry
is in the Lower Peninsula. Both
peninsulas attract tourists who come
to spend vacations in Michigan.

**Read the paragraph. Add headings to
the Venn diagram. Then write facts in
each part of the diagram.**

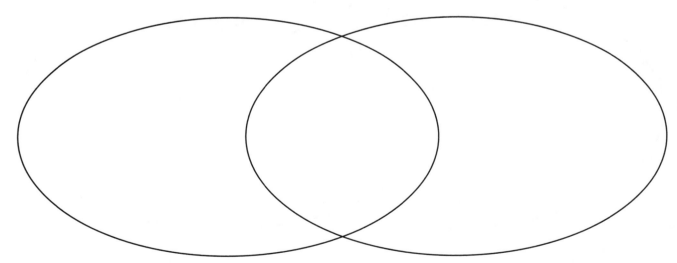

MORE! The Lower Peninsula of Michigan is larger in area than
the Upper Peninsula. Add this fact to the diagram.

Tales of Whales

Scientists divide whales into two groups. The whales in one group have teeth and hunt for food. These are called toothed whales. An example is the killer whale. In the other group are baleen whales. Instead of teeth, these whales have baleen plates in their mouths that act as strainers. When a whale gulps water, any food that floats in stays behind the baleen plates. An example of a baleen whale is the humpback whale. Both groups of whales are mammals.

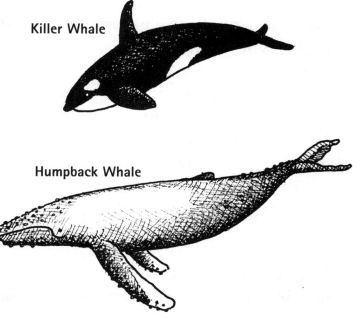

Killer Whale

Humpback Whale

Read the paragraph. Add headings to the Venn diagram. Then write facts in each part of the diagram.

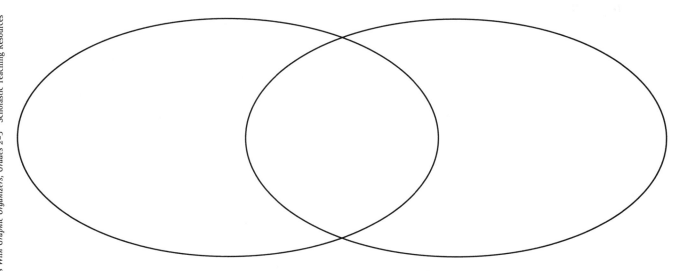

MORE! Find out which group each of the following whales belongs to: rorqual, beluga, narwhal, and blue. Add these whales to the diagram.

Short Reading Passages With Graphic Organizers, Grades 2–3   Scholastic Teaching Resources

Growing Up

Suppose you lived in Egypt 4,500 years ago. How would your life be different? For one thing, you wouldn't go to school. You wouldn't have hair either! Your head would be shaved, except for one lock behind your right ear. You would eat with your fingers instead of forks and knives. On hot nights, you wouldn't have air conditioning. You would sleep on the roof of your home. Not everything would be so different. You would spend time with your family. You might have a pet dog or cat. You would play with toys, such as balls and dolls. And you would enjoy music.

Read the paragraph. Add headings to the Venn diagram. Then write facts in each part of the diagram.

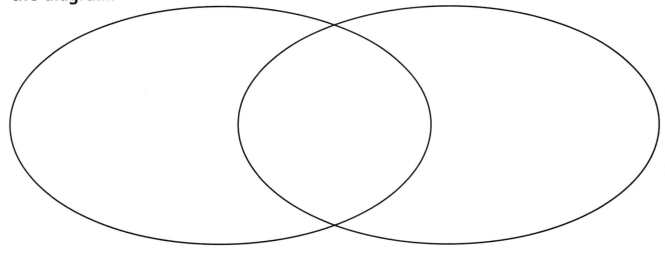

MORE! Long ago, Egyptian children played games, such as tug-of-war, leapfrog, and arm wrestling. Add these facts to the diagram.

Short Reading Passages With Graphic Organizers, Grades 2–3 Scholastic Teaching Resources

Testing It Out

Use after completing Growing Up on page 30.
Fill in the circle of the best answer.

1. Many children in both ancient Egypt and today might—
  (A) play with a cat   (C) play with video games
  (B) ride a bike   (D) go to school

2. Most families today stay cool by—
  (A) going swimming   (C) using air conditioning
  (B) shaving their heads   (D) sleeping outside

3. After dinner, Egyptian children would need to—
  (A) comb their hair   (C) read a book
  (B) wash their hands   (D) write to a friend

4. Children of today—
  (A) have no hair   (C) wear many hair styles
  (B) wear only short hair   (D) have to shave their heads

5. You can guess that most children in ancient Egypt—
  (A) could read and write   (C) had many magazines
  (B) took books out of the library   (D) didn't know how to write

6. Toys such as balls and dolls—
  (A) were not made 4,500 years ago   (C) have been popular for a long time
  (B) are not made today   (D) were only used by ancient Egyptians

7. Both ancient Egyptians and people of today—
  (A) enjoy time with family   (C) eat with knives and forks
  (B) spend time in school   (D) listen to the same music

8. You can guess that most Egyptian homes 4,500 years ago—
  (A) had peaked roofs   (C) were very cool
  (B) had electric fans   (D) were hot at night

Building Blocks

Houses come in many shapes and sizes. They are also built of many different materials. Builders use clay bricks, clay tiles, and clay pipes in many homes. In some parts of the world, grass is used as building material. People weave grasses into mats. They also cover their roofs with grasses. Wood is another common material. Many homes are built of wood planks called clapboard. Wood is also used to make shingles for the roof. Some homes are made of logs, too.

Read the paragraph. Then answer the questions.

1. What are three ways that wood is used? _____

2. What are three ways that clay is used? _____

3. How is grass used in houses? _____

Use your answers to complete the chart.

Wood	Clay	Grasses

MORE! Use your chart to make up a question. Have a classmate answer it.

Short Reading Passages With Graphic Organizers, Grades 2–3   Scholastic Teaching Resources

Play Ball

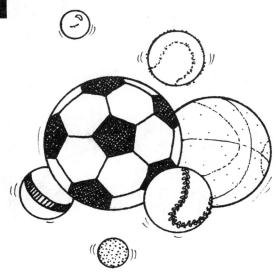

What's your favorite ball game? Many people like sports in which they throw a ball. In bowling and basketball, you throw a ball. Other people play games in which they hit a ball. Golf and tennis are two examples. Still another game in which a ball is hit is lacrosse. A third kind of ball game calls for kicking a ball. Players kick balls in soccer, football, rugby, and, of course, kickball.

Read the paragraph. Then answer the questions.

1. What are four sports where you kick a ball? _____

2. What are three sports in which you hit a ball? _____

3. In what games do you throw a ball? _____

Use your answers to complete the chart.

Hitting a Ball	Throwing a Ball	Kicking a Ball

MORE! What do you do with the ball in baseball? Add baseball to the chart.

Short Reading Passages With Graphic Organizers, Grades 2–3 Scholastic Teaching Resources

Let's Celebrate

People everywhere enjoy holidays. Some celebrations are religious. These include Christmas, Hannukah, and Ramadan. Many holidays such as Thanksgiving celebrate harvests. In India, the Hindu harvest holiday is Pongal. Jewish people celebrate Sukkot. Other holidays are national. In the United States, Independence Day is July 4. In Norway, people celebrate Constitution Day. The French national holiday is Bastille Day.

Read the paragraph. Then answer the questions.

1. Which three national holidays are named? _____

2. Which three religious holidays are named? _____

3. Which harvest holidays are named? _____

Use your answers to complete the chart.

National Holidays	Harvest Holidays	Religious Holidays

MORE! Find another holiday to add to each group on the chart.

Short Reading Passages With Graphic Organizers, Grades 2–3   Scholastic Teaching Resources

Shaping Up

A globe is one. So are oranges and some melons. And don't forget balls. How are these things alike? They are all round shapes called spheres. Two other kinds of shapes are cylinders and cubes. An example of a cylinder is the cardboard tube inside a roll of paper towels. A toy block is an example of a cube. Other examples of cubes are square boxes and ice cubes. Some good examples of cylinders are candles, cans, and straws.

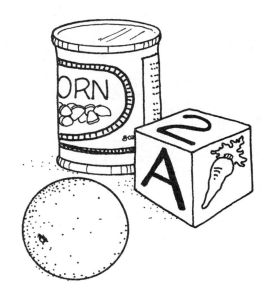

Use the paragraph to write three headings for the chart. Then write examples under each heading.

MORE! Add the following things to the chart: marble, piece of pipe, lipstick.

Bag Tags

Flying to Florida? The tag on your bag will tell what city you're going to. If it's Orlando, the tag will have MCO. For Miami, the tag is MIA. Tampa is TPA, and Ft. Lauderdale is FLL. JAX means you're going to Jacksonville, Florida. But LAX means Los Angeles, California. Other California tags are SAN for San Diego, SFO for San Francisco, and SMF for Sacramento. If you're flying to Texas, your bags might be tagged for these airports— HOU for Houston, SAT for San Antonio, or AUS for Austin. Have a good trip!

Use the paragraph to write three headings for the chart. Then write examples under each heading.

MORE! Add the following airport codes to the chart: SJC (San Jose, California), PBI (West Palm Beach, Florida), SRQ (Sarasota, Florida).

Short Reading Passages With Graphic Organizers, Grades 2–3 Scholastic Teaching Resources

Blending In

How are the following words alike: *blue, black, blink*? If you said they all begin with *bl*, you're right. Some other words that begin with these letters are *blob, blanket,* and *blimp*. Letter pairs like *bl* are blends. Blends are two or more consonants that work together. What blend do the following words begin with: *green, gray, grumpy*? Two other blends are *tr* and *sm*. Words such as *smoke, smile, try, tray, smack, trick, truck,* and *smell* begin with these blends.

Use the paragraph to write four headings for the chart. Then write examples under each heading.

MORE! Add at least two more words to each group on the chart.

Quilts of History

Many quilts tell the story of pioneer life. These patchwork blankets had names with special meanings. Friends often made an album quilt for a family heading West. Each block of the quilt was made and signed by a different friend. Album quilt names include Autograph, Hole in the Barn Door, and Signature. Other quilts, such as North Wind, told the story of weather. Sunburst, Whirlwind, and Weather Vane were other names of weather quilts. What was the trip West like? Quilt names like Hill and Valley, Rocky Glen, and Broken Dishes should give you some idea! Pioneers had fun too. Quilt names such as Wedding Rings, Baby Blocks, Next Door Neighbor, and Friendship Basket suggest special times.

Friendship Basket

Use the paragraph to write four headings for the chart. Then write examples under each heading.

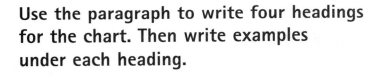

MORE! Use your chart to tell someone about quilt names.

Short Reading Passages With Graphic Organizers, Grades 2–3 Scholastic Teaching Resources

Testing It Out

Use after completing Quilts of History on page 38.
Fill in the circle of the best answer.

1. Quilts are a kind of—

    (A) friendship   (C) blanket

    (B) autograph   (D) neighbor

2. One name of a weather quilt was—

    (A) Broken Dishes   (C) North Wind

    (B) Next Door Neighbor   (D) Hill and Valley

3. Signature and Hole in the Barn Door were examples of—

    (A) special times quilts   (C) weather quilts

    (B) traveling west quilts   (D) album quilts

4. Album quilts were often—

    (A) welcome home quilts   (C) baby gifts

    (B) wedding gifts   (D) going away gifts

5. A quilt that did <u>not</u> tell about special times was—

    (A) Rocky Glen   (C) Friendship Basket

    (B) Wedding Rings   (D) Baby Blocks

6. You can guess that the trip West was—

    (A) always sunny   (C) short and dull

    (B) often bumpy   (D) usually rainy

7. A Sunshine and Shadows quilt would most likely be —

    (A) a special times quilt   (C) an album quilt

    (B) a weather quilt   (D) a going West quilt

8. Two quilt names that tell about the hard trip West are—

    (A) Hill and Valley and Broken Dishes   (C) North Wind and Friendship Basket

    (B) Wedding Rings and Sunburst   (D) Autograph and Weather Vane

Short Reading Passages With Graphic Organizers, Grades 2–3 Scholastic Teaching Resources

Silly Laws

Many states have some silly laws. Usually, these laws were made in the past for a good reason. Over time, the need for the laws changed. Now the laws seem silly. For example, don't let a donkey sleep in your bathtub in Arizona. You might have to pay a fine. Don't whistle underwater in Vermont. You might get put in jail!

Read the paragraph. Answer the questions.
Use your answers to fill in each cause-and-effect map.

1. What could happen if you whistle underwater in Vermont? _____

2. What might cause you to pay a fine in Arizona? _____

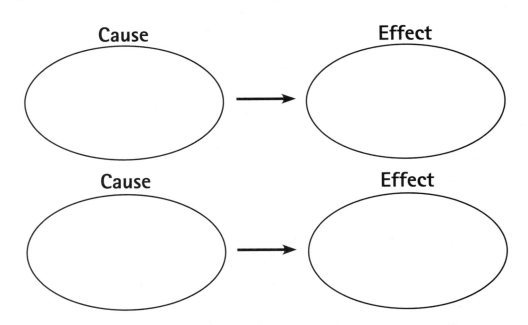

Cause　　　　　　**Effect**

Cause　　　　　　**Effect**

MORE! Don't fish from a camel in Idaho! It's against the law. Make a cause-and-effect map for this law.

Short Reading Passages With Graphic Organizers, Grades 2–3 Scholastic Teaching Resources

Cooling a Kampong

Let's visit a village in Malaysia. Malaysia is a country in Asia. The village, called a kampong, is in a hot, wet jungle. The kampong has no electricity. There is no air conditioning in any of the buildings. People keep their homes cool and dry by building their houses on stilts. Air can blow around the houses.

Read the paragraph. Answer the questions.
Use your answers to fill in each cause-and-effect map.

1. Why do people in the kampong need to cool their houses? _____

2. Why doesn't the kampong have air conditioning? _____

3. What is the effect of building houses on stilts? _____

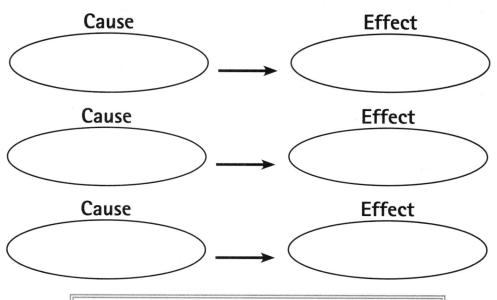

MORE! Find the continent Asia and the country Malaysia on a world map.

Short Reading Passages With Graphic Organizers, Grades 2–3   Scholastic Teaching Resources

Eat and Read

Marty Doyle collected thousands of books. One day, he ran out of room for them. Mr. Doyle took some of the books to the restaurant that he owned. He gave a free book to each diner. As a result, the restaurant soon became famous as a place to eat and read. Other people began giving their extra books to the restaurant, too.

Read the paragraph. Answer the questions.

1. What was Mr. Doyle's problem? _____

2. How did he solve it? _____

3. What two things happened to the restaurant after that? _____

Use your answers to complete the cause-and-effect map.

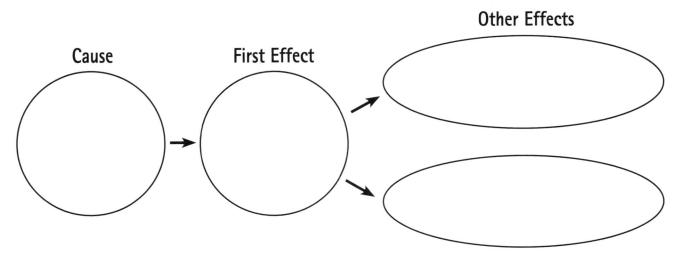

MORE! Draw a picture showing what mealtime at Mr. Doyle's restaurant might look like.

Short Reading Passages With Graphic Organizers, Grades 2–3 Scholastic Teaching Resources

Fool the Birds

A woman in Virginia had a problem. Birds ate all the seeds she carefully planted. The woman put brown belts along the newly planted rows in her garden. Just as she had hoped, the birds thought the belts were snakes! As a result, the birds stayed out of the garden. The woman's plants grew in peace.

Read the paragraph. Then complete the cause-and-effect map.

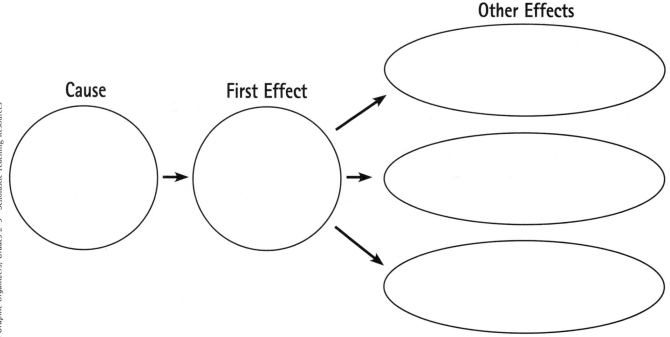

Cause **First Effect** **Other Effects**

MORE! What conclusions can you make about birds and snakes?

Excellent Elephants

Elephants are the largest animals on land. These strong, smart animals live in Africa and parts of Asia. You may have seen elephants in zoos, too. Elephants are in danger of dying out. One reason is that people hunt them for their ivory tusks. There's an even bigger cause why elephants are dying out. The land where elephants live is being taken over by people.

Read the paragraph. Then complete the cause–and–effect map.

Causes

Effect

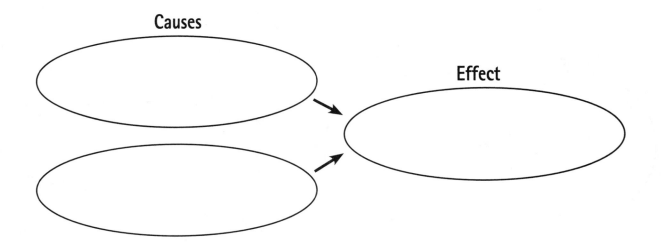

MORE! Learn about the differences between African and Asian elephants. Then make a Venn diagram to show your information.

Short Reading Passages With Graphic Organizers, Grades 2–3 Scholastic Teaching Resources

Where the Sun Shines

Florida is known for its pleasant weather. In fact, it has earned the nickname "Sunshine State." As a result of its warm, sunny climate, Florida is a good place for growing fruits, such as oranges and grapefruits. Many older people go to live in Florida. They enjoy the good weather. Northerners on vacation also visit Florida for the same reason.

Read the paragraph. Then complete the cause-and-effect map.

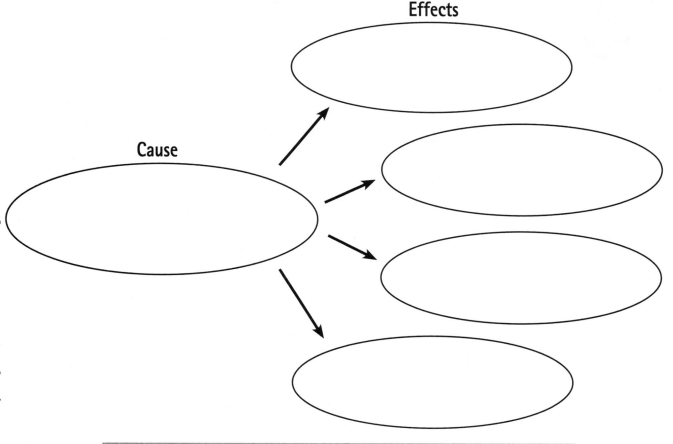

MORE! During which season do most people probably go to Florida? Tell why you think so.

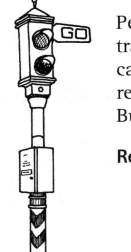

Seeing Red

People really notice the color red. As a result, red is used on traffic lights. The color tells drivers to stop. Brake lights on cars are also red. Emergency exit signs inside buildings are red, too. Because people notice red, it is often used in ads. But too much red in a bedroom can make it hard to sleep.

Read the paragraph. Then complete the cause-and-effect map.

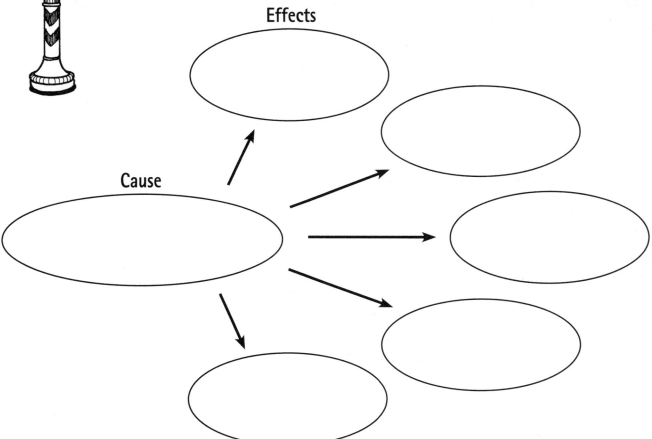

MORE! Explain to someone why red is used in traffic lights.

Testing It Out

Use after completing Seeing Red on page 46.
Fill in the circle of the best answer.

1. Red is used on traffic lights because it—
  Ⓐ is a pretty color   Ⓒ keeps people awake
  Ⓑ makes people notice   Ⓓ means "go ahead"

2. Ads often contain red because—
  Ⓐ the color means danger   Ⓒ the color is easy to read
  Ⓑ people like the color   Ⓓ people notice the color

3. It's important for drivers to—
  Ⓐ see exit signs inside buildings   Ⓒ see brake lights on other cars
  Ⓑ notice red in different ads   Ⓓ use red to stay awake

4. Red is used in emergency exit signs so people will—
  Ⓐ put on their brakes   Ⓒ stop what they're doing
  Ⓑ go to sleep quickly   Ⓓ see the signs easily

5. The paragraph does not say that—
  Ⓐ brake lights are red   Ⓒ red tells drivers to stop
  Ⓑ people notice the color red   Ⓓ people "see red" when they are angry

6. You can guess that too much red might—
  Ⓐ make it easy to sleep   Ⓒ cause drivers to brake
  Ⓑ make it hard to nap   Ⓓ cause people to stay inside a building

7. You can guess that fire engines are red because—
  Ⓐ it is a popular color   Ⓒ people will see them and get out of the way
  Ⓑ firefighters like the color red   Ⓓ it matches their brake lights

8. The paragraph suggests that red is a—
  Ⓐ useful color   Ⓒ calm color
  Ⓑ dull color   Ⓓ favorite color

Short Reading Passages With Graphic Organizers, Grades 2–3 Scholastic Teaching Resources

Answers

Accept all reasonable answers.

Page 6: 1. willow 2. salute 3. comet

Page 7: 1. islands 2. blueberries 3. lobster

Page 8: 1. half a pound 2. 60 miles an hour 3. 10 to 15 years

Page 9: crust, mantle, outer core, inner core

Page 10: Arizona state colors are blue and gold; South Carolina state amphibian is the salamander; North Dakota state drink is milk; Maine state insect is the honeybee; Massachusetts state dessert is Boston cream pie.

Page 11: laugh—16 mph; yawn—9 mph; snore—6-7 mph; hiccup—50 mph; sneeze—104 mph

Page 12: topic: Favorite Sandwiches for School Lunches; details: peanut butter and jelly; ham; bologna; cheese; turkey

Page 13: topic: U.S. Symbols; details: flag; Uncle Sam; Statue of Liberty; Liberty Bell; bald eagle

Page 14: topic: Different Cars Carry Different Things; details: Locomotive carries engineer; Hopper car carries coal, sand, salt; Flatcar carries large things that must be tied down; Tanker car carries gas; Boxcar carries many things; Caboose carries offices and beds for crew.

Page 15: 1. B 2. B 3. B 4. A 5. D 6. B 7. C 8. A

Page 16: 1. Smoke came out of the sea. 2. Red-hot rock poured down its sides. 3. The volcano cooled down. 4. The new island was named Surtsey.

Page 17: 1. Fires were built on hillsides. 2. Candles were used. 3. Oil lamps lit lighthouses. 4. Lighthouses use electric light.

Page 18: 1. The cranes come to the Platte River. 2. The cranes eat and rest. 3. The cranes fly to the far north. 4. The mating season begins.

Page 19: 1. Four boys go out with their dog. 2. Robot gets lost. 3. The boys hear barking and climb into a hole. 4. The boys find cave paintings. 5. The cave paintings become very famous.

Page 20: 1. no can opener at picnic 2. decides there must be a better way 3. invents pop-top 4. invents push-in, fold-back top

Page 21: 1. whistle 2. rocking horse 3. bike 4. crayons 5. video games

Page 22: 1. drawings done 2. models made 3. cut out and put together pieces 4. blow up and paint balloons

Page 23: 1. C 2. D 3. B 4. B 5. D 6. B 7. C 8. D

Page 24: Car Ferry—carries cars, has ramps; Both—cross water, carry vehicles, 330 feet long; Train Ferry—carries trains, has tracks

Page 25: Beech—uneven edges, turn orange-brown; Both—long, narrow leaves; Black Gum—smooth edges, turn yellow

Page 26: Japan—white background, circle for sun; Both—red and white; Canada—white background with two red stripes, red maple leaf

Page 27: South Pole—on continent of Antarctica, scientists study rocks and ice; Both—very cold, six months of day and six months of night; North Pole—in Arctic Ocean, no land, no one makes home there

Page 28: Upper Peninsula—big forests, minerals; Both—attract tourists, part of Michigan, surrounded by Great Lakes; Lower Peninsula—more people and large cities, most of industry

Page 29: Toothed Whales—have teeth and hunt, killer whale; Both—mammals; Baleen Whales—baleen plates, humpback

Page 30: Ancient Egypt—no school, shave hair, eat with fingers, sleep on roof; Both—spend time with family, play with balls and dolls, like music, have pets; Today—school, many hairstyles, use forks and knives, have fans and air conditioning

Page 31: 1. A 2. C 3. B 4. C 5. D 6. C 7. A 8. D

Page 32: Wood—clapboard, shingles, logs; Clay—bricks, tiles, pipes; Grasses—mats, to cover roofs

Page 33: Hitting a Ball—golf, tennis, lacrosse; Throwing a Ball—basketball, bowling; Kicking a Ball—soccer, football, rugby, kickball

Page 34: National Holidays—Independence Day (U.S.), Constitution Day (Norway), Bastille Day (France); Harvest Holidays—Thanksgiving (U.S.), Pongal (India), Sukkot (Jewish); Religious Holidays—Christmas, Hannukah, Ramadan

Page 35: Spheres—oranges, melons, balls, globes; Cubes—blocks, boxes, ice cubes; Cylinders—paper towel tubes, candles, cans, straws

Page 36: Florida—MCO (Orlando), MIA (Miami), TPA (Tampa), FLL (Ft. Lauderdale), JAX (Jacksonville); California—LAX (Los Angeles), SAN (San Diego), SFO (San Francisco), SMF (Sacramento); Texas—HOU (Houston), SAT (San Antonio), AUS (Austin)

Page 37: BL—blue, black, blink, blob, blanket, blimp; GR—green, gray, grumpy; TR—try, tray, trick, truck; SM—smoke, smile, smack, smell

Page 38: Album Quilts—Autograph, Hole in the Barn Door, Signature; Weather Quilts—North Wind, Sunburst, Whirlwind, Weather Vane; Going West Quilts—Hill and Valley, Rocky Glen, Broken Dishes; Special Times Quilts—Wedding Rings, Baby Blocks, Next Door Neighbor, Friendship Basket

Page 39: 1. C 2. C 3. D 4. D 5. A 6. B 7. B 8. A

Page 40: Cause—whistle under water in Vermont, Effect—arrest; Cause—let donkey sleep in tub in Arizona, Effect—fine

Page 41: Cause—hot climate, Effect—need to cool houses; Cause—no electricity, Effect—no air conditioning; Cause—houses on stilts, Effect—air can blow around to cool homes

Page 42: Cause—ran out of room for books; First Effect—took books to restaurant and gave one to each diner; Other Effects—restaurant became famous, people gave their extra books

Page 43: Cause—birds eating seeds; First Effect—put brown belts in garden; Other Effects—birds thought belts were snakes, birds stayed away from garden, plants grew in peace

Page 44: Causes—elephants hunted for ivory, humans taking over land; Effect—elephants in danger of dying out

Page 45: Cause—Florida has warm, sunny climate; Effects—called "Sunshine State," good for growing oranges and grapefruit, older people go to live there, vacationers visit there

Page 46: Cause—red is attention-getting color; Effects—used on traffic lights, brake lights, emergency exit lights, used in ads, makes it hard for people to sleep

Page 47: 1. B 2. D 3. C 4. D 5. D 6. B 7. C 8. A